I0210682

Bottomland

Laressa Dickey

Bottomland

Shearsman Books

First published in the United Kingdom in 2014 by
Shearsman Books
50 Westons Hill Drive
Emersons Green
BRISTOL
BS16 7DF

Shearsman Books Ltd Registered Office
30–31 St. James Place, Mangotsfield, Bristol BS16 9JB
(this address not for correspondence)

www.shearsman.com

ISBN 978-1-84861-326-3

Copyright © Laressa Dickey, 2014.
The right of Laressa Dickey to be identified as the author
of this work has been asserted by her in accordance with the
Copyrights, Designs and Patents Act of 1988.
All rights reserved.

ACKNOWLEDGEMENTS

'A Pictorial History of Wilderness' and 'Mimesis, Synaptic' were published as
chapbooks by MIEL Books, UK, 2012.
'American Rough-leg' no 1-5 appear in *Newfound Journal*.
No 6 appears in 111O/1.
from 'A Pictorial History of Wilderness': 'A voice lifts the music', 'Child of the
west', and 'Night herons quickly lift as felled trees', appear in
Cerise Press, Vol 3, Issue 7.
'Catalogue of Utilities' no 2, 3, and 4 appear in *Referential Magazine*.
No 5 appears in *CURA*, Issue 4.
from 'Route to Cloudless, Day', no 1, 3 and 5 appear online
in *U City Review* (Dec 2012).
'Devotion' & 'Spool' appeared in *Dislocate*, Issue 2.
'Mesmerism' appeared in *Permafrost*, Summer, 2008, Volume 30.
'Blue-tick' appeared in *Konundrum Engine Literary Review*.
'Homicide' appeared in *The Southern Women's Literary Review*.
'Fidelity' and 'Espalier' appeared in *U City Review*, November 2012.
'Sophia' appeared in *The Pinch*, 2013.
'except' and 'between' appeared in *The Museum of Americana*, 2013
'among' appeared in *inter|rupture.*, 2013.
'after' is forthcoming in *Blood Orange Review*.

Contents

for my mother, for my father, for my brother

American Rough-Leg

1

In the dark barn, the real result.
Stripped the tinny tobacco leaves off the split stalk, hand by hand.
For if I lost my feet there. No settling up.
Now, everything in Paris tastes salty. The still rain.
There's the dry leaf crackle, there's diligence.
What is better than the willow branch bending?
You sort yourself out, what doesn't come from cotton.
Tomahawk hatchet, croissant. On the bobbing river or in the row.
Cutting into the sap. Undulate is what her spine does
she dances. Washes salt off her plate.
Everything coming in this back door rushes me.

2

Someone holds the heels. Every hard ankle is touched in the way of welcome. What wind would tell us if the feet are fixed or whether the spine will twirl the body in two. If you are here—I knew the neighbor's stars over his place better than my own. Is this a man keeping order. Is this the body by satellite. Was the impossible thing awake, to board or cage, *oh come on*. To say my reluctance, a bridle; she had more to do by my count—My loss loss showed, following a dentist drill or hydraulic engine. It all came by diesel, anyhow. Just another warning with stripes around the wrists. Unison: I move in the rhythm I like, this hand battering or her glass bones. What means has the heart; a force by which the horse rises up. Is this a sturdy bit or the relevance of the dish falling from her hands

3

Left on Locust. Rick expanded his BBQ joint. A man blowing air slowly his tense lips. Left, Locust. The flea market wasn't for her; he is making pots to sell. Full of Lucy, plinth. So wrong she carried it folded up like a love note, one place she was walking home. He lost the farm, almost, the mint by the creek the bank owns.

You don't want—passive feast. Keep it with you, if my gut would let me, swollen beside the house shifting. O but she waited, feet out over bed; he was static and they situated where I left the hatched locust drying. Hickory trees kicking doors to get out.

4

In the photograph, his grandmother sat on the moon. She resembled dotted daisies, ticked by blushing. Not a moment too soon the red haw. Condense. The family crossed for sixty-eight dollars a person, onerous now her garland nose. They told her all the faults, bay to exhaust the loved, dripping faucet. Before her hands brush her skirt, *will this soothe my new permanent.*

5

For what yes the day begins

His back, I can tell if bright blue signals the garbage truck

To start work if the what wasn't beeping

Endless dimensions won't match these tucked behind the ear words

My double wheel, an image panting

Sudden black squirrel, as if I remember black

Pileated woodpecker in a body of light on a distant oak

The distance is inside me and viscous

6

Here's a cloud deciding to decide the place marked *birds for boys*, small Japanese plates: things politicians are not scared of. Fast you scared of uzi at your nose, just above the Superman pajama neck. You drown on fever. A cold blooming in your left hip. Bothered by the tip of memory you carried its stench on your clothes.

Tonight above your pillow in a room bulging with the disappointment of your mother line. To you she speaks an old language.

Out of war the hair falls, and the sister's. Of the felled and shriveled, pretend the lines, the ones on their faces, smooth to your touch. I am sorry this is not a story where she stands at the window and twirls the curtain in her fingers.

If I say one word I may mean *o my heart* or *o my monster*!

You were elevated by trains I had not seen.

7

Grasslands came before man, coal swamps before reptiles. Avian,
then floral. A million years pressed to stone, as lips, as fins. See: fish
specialized for life in quiet waters. Some stories are shapes burned
together. The tongue a torch on fire, remember it as a planked
platform. We bisect the street, slip fingers out of mittens. Tiny
photographs of your turning wrist we piece together. Somewhere a
shallow field lobbing rockets, agrees with its verb here, to kill, as if.

8

I take trips around the world to dream in all the places. I make the prosperous dictionary of images. Keeper of skin, silent, elemental. I go bald as the old man and know the lay before I arrive. Where starvation no longer haunts. The singing springs from my pores. Following ancient, woe. Quietly a necessary task, rivals I carry in a bundle, befuddled. It is silence cloaks my whereabouts. Lost is misunderstanding yes or no. I prepare myself four times, I stutter and swag.

9

where the heron/has her nest... HD

Who has the healer gone
I took apart the night, stalled it   spinning

Beckon green grass
conceal the last time look—   bare-branched tree

Wine, spill or have them see
dripped over the border   young soldier

On the film to fly
eyes down eyes
apart from night

Drip over *why did they*

Jeweled turquoise on her breast
open as I knew

I flew   if to call the dogs

pissing   dressed a heron nest

Outside, inside the skin

what you know didn't they tell you

What has incensed in it

hot, you remember—
it is a word

10

For those who walk out of deadened grass pretending they know how to pronounce *Schopenhauer*, let me say, *I'll have hands like old knobs*. Now I have drawn my life as a map from birth to death, just where sea becomes forest. Never, until now, have I existed apart from this cordial song. The face of someone my mother would trust. What little time we live. Never, before now, has light circled above me—Please open the door, we'll grow like 17-year-old locust. Never has there existed a door. We'll be cold. This, spring; this the little we have. They say let big winds carry. Never before have I heard this song for so many distances.

Bottomland

Espalier

From above, the land only patterns, lines of which connote movement. This does not equal progress. Instead the language in which they told it, with bodies rather than folded girth. To see the body plainly, in a space commanding attention—this need to understand. Punk, honey. When I play cards, I put my hands behind my head between tricks like my father did when he played Rook. Moving becomes what we repeat but stands for someone else. People whose gestures live inside us. To say some impulse won't be remembered, to lose one's roads and streets, this short welcoming of the world to its people, as in I cannot be a worker, I cannot be a father. My plan is hollowing and atavistic friendships, a tolerance for nothing to do with my own hands.

Sophia

First, to be tentative, then to feel old inside—

Some other mother holding the world

For some, passageways are always women weeping

These rivers your mother didn't build

The maze was colored language
—dust born from the tiny script your fingers made

Children come home and birds—yes,

even there, your grandmother spoke to you.
Who can be this guarded? You were Mary

Your name on the walls of a place where saints walked

Scuffed shoes against a sidewalk   your curses

Which blood will the rain bleed

What used to be church is now only waiting

above the candles, stairs toward a retractable sky

You were some Jesus

Umbrella in hand, world in other

Ninety-five percent of what she says
and only small gestures

Fidelity

In the evenings, my mother stripped my father's socks, rubbed his cracked heels & stinking feet. Because she snored, he slept in a room at the far end of the house. Wore earplugs. When they had guests, she blew up an air mattress and slept on the floor beside him. Always the next day he was tired, tired. The one night of my childhood when my mother wasn't sleeping at home: her father's heart attack, so she slept in a hospital waiting room. I remember: curtain folds in my back, moon-peeks, darkest night of the year. I once heard my father say the word *fuck* in reference to my mother. *That fucking woman,* he said. I was loyal to an old Jerry Lee Lewis record & wore it out one summer. Shake the dumpster, shake it out. Nothing returns, not ankle bones nor ripped strips of memory.

Spool

Before the first sand spilling into your eye
Before the tunnel in the dream, the one you shoot down—
hands out grasping slick-earthed walls, the one that
ends in a thick bed of grass, you, face
up to wind and the song of the world—
Before the thread that you trace back to sleep
Before the winding, the lined
and stacked circles, the sleep of light reflected off slick bone
Inside, we kept spinning: sand, earth, small
glow a gift of the fingers twitching
Into the heart comes the dream of all that is. Stitch
elocute, loop. The knot is how we'll tell
where we are in the night, and underneath
the workings of our very nimble hands

Blue-tick

In the way the wind often does, in the way

the wind and often, does it not appear
often on a dirt lined hand, does it appear

that a hand, a dirt grind, ground in
like hands, not pauses, but hands
linked in dirt in the way the wind

appears, in that   way

My right hand on the same side as yours

In the corner opposite me, angle within
an angle. How things don't touch, and the space

between them hums,   charges. How the space
takes the form of a hand, leftover

shaking itself of hello, goodbye

right on the same side as you

*

The quiet tonight. In my hand
moving toward this heart

the wind and often, does it not appear

breath, the hand reminding
buy saltines, touch somebody's face

Hands are days when I forget the lash of silk

We knew   everything

*

Often on a dirt-lined hand, does it appear
what passed between tabletop and drawer

What god is not, fingered in my front pocket
Change. But yes, when you said I was
removed from my own feelings, I went
looking   my whole life

Braided gate. We put the red mare down
Foot. What appears to put down

What grows toward home? The season
for passage. Time shuffling
a stiff deck. Who kept score   I'm
not recalling

Toss the corner over   you   shoulder
The way the wind often I thought

*

That yearn is not young, but close. Horseshoes
around a ring

like a wooden neck; like cheese

holes for small fingers, for tongues and teeth

The way home hung in the air around

our hands, felt something like hands

like pauses in dirt

Between

I have not said my prayers. My god is tired and lonely. Dressed to
see him, I am lonely too. My brother makes pecan pies and wears a
blue hat. In the corner, our mother murmurs the prayer of the 7th
horse and rolls a penny along the slanting floor. No one comes to
talk with me. That boy snaps his fingers, tap dances to *The Night
Hank Williams Came to Town*. A long time ago, our mother saw
a portrait of a woman who reminded her of an orphan, someone
she knew and could not save. I have never said enough prayers.
My god rolls around in the back of a pickup. Our mother stomps
mushrooms with her open hands and they puff out smoke. No one
tells me it's time to eat.

Devotion

That, and the heart can be bisected. Not then
or now. Something closer to the twist of rope:

catalyst. Some people find hope in dreams
live in between small rock crevices. Down

this road, the day sings. The song of the world
in a lizard's squabble

Call this the place before rain

Although the passengers sleep. A song
in the corner, slow whish

of air conditioning mixing with hum.
One eyelid open near the front. A child flapping

an arm onto the lap of someone not
his father; it won't matter

It is the song itself that sleeps in me

*

Small winged things. Why should you be surprised

I witness the between of dragonfly, damselfly and what is neither

Too long I've sung a strange refrain
Mostly trained extravagance to stay away

What surprised me: how slow we walk
what burns the tongue

*

What happens when devotion is eclipsed?

What becomes of? The wind in the tin of the tree-top;
photographs pieced together with fingernail polish.

This is what I looked for in the dream and found: small heart

threaded through the place before

After

My grandmother tells a story. One that came from under her bed, where she hid her cigarettes and where the stuffed dog played through the night. You were once under the pillow dear, she begins. A large wolf howled. Some mice said grace and threw rice. You cried and who could help laughing at you—the hot water burning your legs. You were once a pincushion—that's when you were particularly useful. We picked our teeth with needles. Sometimes we travel in the story. First there was a boat, and the family was in it, and you were on the tallest building looking for snails. We called for you, but you hid from us. We looked for you under lily pads, in holly berries.

Among

Time to walk my dead. Time to clutch their landless hands in my elbow garden so they won't shudder and shit those government-issued overalls. I treat them like lost lambs, seventy-two since the last trip; once we slosh in the creek—long ribbon of gray-eyed fledglings tied to my ribs with rubber strings—we'll tour the local dog cemetery & look for Butch, Clyde & Poochie. They welcome these afternoon walks, where I show them the triptych in the back woods: one part rotten deer-stand, one part quail coveys in concentric circles, broken fence crossings. By now, they've snitched all their stories. So I grill them like lifeless 8-balls. Blood slithers past my toothless future. Did you get your own room? Is it quiet there? Blink three times if you're certain there's love left for me.

Homicide

What we store inside: old weightlifting equipment, rusted tools on nails in the sitting room. Two tombstones from Charlotte Ann and William Ray's graves. Early logs date from 1831, but who built this house? Once the doctor disjoints the oldest logs, once the house is gutted in this way. What we call it: homicide. In the kitchen, the paint peels in strips like tall grass. This is what we will forget: the births of this house, my grandmother's collection of small porcelain shoes, aunts and uncles, 7 dogs, 21 cats, various chickens, feeder pigs, 4 horses (Old Cole among them). The house will suck in, fall apart. Remember the rosy wallpaper. Keep in mind the winding steps to the secret room. That tub of lard. Under the sink, newspapers from 1903. The old TV in the far corner. Remember the crooked man peering over his horn-rimmed glasses and puffing a pipe: my grandfather. See the smoke rise up and circle his head?

Except

They called me little Jimmy, short but I swung my limbs like nobody. My fingers torn to bits from the welding arc but I still pluck that banjo, sell quail to those who want birds to hunt or sing. I jammed all my sockets into this blasted life my mama gave me. I tore it up and forgot. My life is higher up the hill from here; routine drumming its fingers on my scull. This is the old place they bought fastened to dark in bottomland. One sorry line after another, a man with worn out work gloves. This bailing twine. I spit and win contests. Where did you cut your teeth, they ask me and I say my mama put coffee in the baby bottle. I am solid when I reach back but all the woods are stony.

Mesmerism
—for Aldo Leopold

not unmindful of my obligation to these

Mother of us all, mother woman, woman

moon, falling feather.

Window woman, spell maker, heart stitcher. Plucker

of limbs, finger licker—

here's to the limits of the arrow.

in my mind so long that I cannot recall just when or
how

Glass bowl woman, translucent Elvis lamp woman,

stone singer, javelin spirit, sunken.

Swim in the river of this mother of god.

Like the river, he disappeared.

How intricate her mouth was, even when

she grew older. It pinched itself and her yellowed

teeth like a corn harvest, seemed as sweet.

Catalogue of Utilities

1

Ah, the tamarind, remember the way they say, "tree of life." We wound its leaves around our fingers, took their shadows for bird feet. Ah, the open mouthed fish, especially children to love the day. They move without clicking joints. You also moved from some within. O fingers, you dig, O roots. If you are charmed as you are charmed by schools of koi. I wasn't going anywhere though the day was green and families from foreign places were out adventuring, I wasn't one. Bitter things scratch. It was late and I don't know why I remembered tamarind. As if we were still local. And if we chewed sugar cane. The blessed clicking again. Then *shhhhh* as fish bodies surface. A murmur of words from another place.

The siblings of the sun emerge from the mirror of the sky.

Powder, dust, run butterfly, and rain. The quarter turn of the nurse's skirt she checks ears. Imagine hearing unhappiness become the clomping of frogs. Opens some door in another country with more frequent sun. *Cows with names make more milk.* Who can focus thoughts in this weather, if fire the measure of steadiness, build it. Catch no nap, if he's napping. Her country the intruding persistence at her belly. Take up indefinite words, cover. Say we made this, while sitting under blossomed tree outside the children's cancer ward; it was a poem he spoke if I wrote it down.

3

For shapes fit in the mouth, do they thank you, thin and wiry. You would bend and say hello to them, because they could be exotic. I wish I were a fog with a point on top. Listen, if I say *they might eat*, just look at their mouths. I stick my hands in, I can hold it, a great idea. Walk each leaf. Treat as if by accident they are right here calling you; don't you have food for them? Why did they go to water? You were something before you were a statue. They greet me and huddle. *How are you*, whispered as she bends to see herself. Where has her mind gone? She has focused her frown.

4

If then, you are to believe this—You must also count the wind inside scorn. For if by the way you stand, huskily, over the bodies. Shrink, if you need to, the liver-fastening pill of your madness. If you mean impossible, think of the mountain. You love it but mimic its inertia. Body edible, not spirit. Where someone stares, it's only to fix the memory of sun tinting off teapot in their high street house. Dangerous body, danger in bending. *The soul, goes wherever.* Where do you, plain sight. Take Bangladesh, whom you offended and come into this world, civility.

5

Even in her long shadow she won't dance. If the din of what moves moves. The fort where she laughs and what fills. You I'm sorry I can't touch. He is 10. His grandfather mumbles about the fish. A rubber tree. I remember something when I come here. Magnolia, an old woman's sour linens. Grandmother's neighbor, Katherine. All this work in life, nailed to a white wall, outlined, but what flower does it smell like? This messy life not branded. How does it keep dividing? Instead of a division, say, this coat is heavy.

6

Before, she was the lady making family, a turned implement for torsos. Work stacked, lined slough, wrinkled. The flight wave of the finch cheers. Something felt ochre on my tongue, two children on the bed jumping. Green, *so long.* If I come nearer than my body to you, do ask permission to wrap the head in white. Sing, do I wink do you flee. How close the close beside you, play beside yes what if we flail. To know by noodling around the mulberry the arc of long thumb. What evolved from maple leaves in the gutters, how to get to Tokyo from our own house.

A Pictorial History
of Wilderness

...Where his heel came down again and again...
—Philip Levine

A voice lifts the music, a whisper shaped like a person in this room
and he's talking to me

Do not anchor—this list of what you made while you waited

All you dreamed from the seasonal arrival of a Sears catalog.
Light is opening the fronds, see

the ticket counter where you speak
your destination and realize you might say any place

If I sleep here, isn't this a story. The voice of someone whose voice
is glimmering, trumpet, vine

The iris expands to take in. Appears here

whaling blue night

                              What is lighting everything

Inordinate amount of solitary birch, you lean out

Might as well be the end of the earth. All my spaces went from two
to one. Enter the red berries, cluster. Across bird, strips of freezing
rain

One loses many senses. Traveling medicine shows

Some server's brought joy in on small, stacked dishes

you call her

yes, you call, on the phone or with your fingers do they still work
yes with her number, do you remember the butterfly wings and
pants you ripped on rebar—

it was some place and we were some place mad at each other

We would like two, we would please request, yes and next door
they put a window in the apex and glass prism

afterwards they built a whole house around it

Why say wilderness when you mean body, or glove
Parsimonious speech is bitter as if floating above taste

The family told stories over and over, an active remembering

When our neighbor Phillip shot himself one morning before work
did his right hand know what his left had done

We waited for the school bus, ambulance passed

I cannot say something here about pleasure

If you weren't raised that way, what would that way be—

Down glance on the path to avoid bright moss in crumbling leaves

Who stacked pebbles on top of each other, meaning why is that ship
sailing so close to my own shore. A natural history forgets
to mention mergansers

Tinctures produce the ability to look down into the heart

Each wind seemed to take the curved surface   farther out
while the blue   floated in

The river running away from me

                                        Perturbed geese
they fly. Swans taking off
                        sputtering crank motor

Hold me, repeating gravestones in snow

Gloat the way folks build houses facing the water

Is this thing holy. *Twenty thirty forty-five*

Of all the people passing through our card playing

Did I take my pills. I stayed home though   it was fair we
changed places

                                Before I had only been to Florida

Saw two eagles beside the memory of cactus and thought *odd*

Child of the west, if as I, you speak a milky crane

Seen under water the bathing place for stone

Rare herons spotted here but do we make the trip   I hunted
the dictionary of all mammals.

We ate mackerel out of a can, mashed together in patties and fried,
large as a child's palm

Did we come from the place I loved for its low dousing of clouds

Night herons quickly lift as felled trees

Seven days and all the doves on our windowsills quiver

They have come in color, tricked by winter's shadow

Today snow fell and fell again to thicken

This dawn sleeping by a mother's breast it is not mine

Pieces of land lay beside each other, we look for edges that fit easily

The body not machine, some ground to till or pick rocks out of

The world's tallest building within the shape of a hand when it is
no longer yours

O June! Remember the tiny basket of bulbs, remember the cheek
Were her shoulders fluttering

Who said the arms fly both ways

I had fun dialing your number. Absolutely you sing—if you
forget to piece together the red fabric, stacked silk

Approach your lost sleep when you eat like sugar. Or markets

where I cracked a tooth and all the stalls the same: car parts,
a booth of tires, one for chains or engines or fenders.

     Quarter the parts, the fly into the owner's sleeping mouth.
Is that man chewing his own foot

A veil or flowerpot on your head

Then the upside down cartwheel. I am still tired!

Down working in the woods, sweet in the back of my throat
I wondered if my body would soften

Late in the night swindles of hair twined where you have run your
fingers through
                                    They stand in corners
and give direction. Wanting to get outside for the crunched now

so I called the body a cocklebur

Haircuts, a mark for the way a family remembers itself. Mom, my cat, mom, my cat; yes, yes

I like to remember him by his honey jars

To learn his language, would I lose some placement inside myself

All told, the heart expands, and hair, these given

we learn to talk by other talkings

A boy with big eyes given a careful assignment

What music he loved

Route to Cloudless, Day

1

If the mind inside the body blackens does the body blacken

In sleep, his memory flaps like a threatened bird

When each night before bed she eats banana with warmed milk

He can't explain why he's incredulous

For a time he didn't know he had a memory because of the size of other memories

How did I know fingers crossed behind my back were good luck or lying

She didn't remember she didn't remember, so continuously fed the horse bananas

The young get angry when the old can't recall names of streets

After all, daughters remember less

As if I've swallowed the sun, she says, worst I've ever felt

I would like to sustain this action as if to say the body teaches the mind about itch

Somewhere, if someone sleeps

2

A man gazes out the airport window, the fog his old ocean
Of the game he played in dusty fields
Initially light, then jostled noise
Was he running toward third base, is this too-big coat holding
    his shoulders
Whose feet, what hardened joints, socket
His cards bear a full name, but here at the window
it's his grandmother calling—

                    Here's how to prune the rose, so it blooms full
For instance, she wasn't one to smile, mouth crouched behind
    tiny fingers
Sore hand, she spoke over waves. He could hear water from an
    outdoor faucet

The old woman warning of the bite believes her child's teeth will be
strong but the child will think trees were bigger once

As the leaves he saw not moved by wind, but in concert with
frequencies— so what stirred them also shimmered his memory

3

A horse's eyes full of flies. Not up in the air anymore. A child of the child, she is not barren. Take it in the teeth, a fatty place I squeezed my own eyes shut when I laughed at nine. My burning heart, dear. Suddenly I couldn't be like me. If this is what it's like to be fertile and produce a child as with-child friends would. This doll you cannot play with. Round up the whole gang, so much empty, all sentence. And the day faking sunset. He is black but his lips are black.

4

Some talk about weather and the hungry way you pucker your mouth. Obvious fortune and sturdy woe, she broke the horse. I stand, now, as people for whom we switch places. The couch imprint on my face just the known observable wonder. This farm is a freeze of complaints and dreams thinly sliced. I bake your welcome, now stale crust I hold inside, were it autumn. If only he felt in some way useful or brought me salt pork. In the next room, her body slacks, for example, the grandmother who will eat me. Yesterday, to walk far the rain lulled *remember this body scattering inside you—* If my arms carried her long grey hair wound where it had been joined. A memory pinched like piecrust. It's obvious she flew into the first day, my form the twined rope she fingered. I swallowed I wandered, just tell me as I spit into. The blue manner of her stacked bowls—one outwits the wind. Nip, for cough or bud. I sing opulent, otherwise, *you kill the bird, you kill the song.* Now I thank a simmering pot, hate the chewing beside me. My first legs and I begged her to let me shave them.

Culled, I walked through.

5

O beloved. This mayhem costuming the skeletal of my once.

I'm simply what I don't know interrupting

so badly to cry,

                                A fine enough delineation with big eyes

a knocking door;
man carrying his pumping heart

Remember my name as it comes to you through window glass

we knew angels, breaking
its order

                If we touch what we think,   *kaputt!*
empty pillars, he felt joy in his limbs

If   I
had said

                                and you nodded

my how the architecture

                        recedes

Mimesis, synaptic

His mother said he put his ear to the ground when he was scared. I stood across the café from him when this happened. We were lost, but then I crossed the room to put my ear down. It cost fifty cents, but it cost. *Let it groove on its own thing.* A small candy, a room where she was born, and he held her. Later, he would hold her body and their own child inside his crossed arms. Wasn't he the only one who could ask us why we weren't married?

Three monks in tangerine robes walk in rain the market's length. A young man in jeans straddling a silver bicycle leans toward them. Each step they step they step to gravity. *I didn't have time for birds when I was young.* A man riding a red motorcycle wearing a sky-blue poncho passes. The sky negligible from where we stand. When night comes, the colors will quicken, tangle.

Wind chill blows the crocus off its root. When will the women in this hollow speak to each other? Even Rosie the dog has died. A small piece of land easily moves certain surfaces. When clouds relocate, and creek water quiets. Birches snap in two. When gales skirt down hills, maybe then. The sounds aren't recognizable, until someone translates. *What you say is poetry if you mean what you say.*

Men on power lines and transformer towers. Are they red-shouldered hawk or fair-weathered? Pieces of tin peeled off barns and rolled neatly into cylinder ditch sculpture. Look at my brother stand in my Easter dress. Later, his big arms with ax lift trees from across the road. This half-head pain a sleep in the field of gravity. Strong, early light. Get dressed in the pleasant skirt you used to wear, you blend, you bring the body.

Every book a man book. In 1983, Matt Martin jabbed a pencil into the flesh above my left knee, and you fled your country at night by plane instead of mountain. I had seen neither but felt the blood ooze down my leg as I peeped toward Ms. Ingram *for God's sake*. In the middle of her clicking compact and lipstick measuring. My words coiled in the keel of my breastbone.

Cover the mind with a hat. Is it here (*point to heart*) or here (*point to pelvis*)? You can't keep saying you ate mackerel out of a can, or that your father made popcorn in a cast iron skillet on the stove. Every evening duties persist. Where do these movements come from?

The man sitting in the corner of room darkened except for the flickering light of pro wrestling on TV. Is he lost chewing the end of his pipe? A book, propped on his knees. Were we outside, in an old metal lawn chair sunk back with the sitter. All this impartial. I smelled rust.

The world catches fire with the grandfather

The book might have been the alphabet. Daffodils, the odd squirming spine, too still too long, too near. Flaps of fake brick siding, pack of hounds and inbred sheepdogs flocking, now skunk, now red bird. Flowering vine across eves, fluttering possibilities in too-tall grass.

Was there an orchard behind us? I liked the low-branched peach trees, sparse. They had once been something. Careless lazing branch of oak beside us, we all in full sun. Often, he brought objects inside the house to show us: wild Muscatine grape cluster, cat skull, newborn kitten curled in his palm.

Gravity teaches the spine's length. Femur, long bones. I said something I couldn't contain the contents of. Report back to you and outdo the boys. Inside, the right combination of vinegar and cucumbers floating in the kitchen sink. Whip around to your Bruce Lee loving brother and avoid the too-close roundhouse kicks. All the weather to hide in her way. Did she love the cricket? Vernal rocket of her hair but nothing happens. Just say where you go if you know. Some cult of loneliness this is.

Thanks

So many people had a hand in supporting me in the creation of Bottomland. I would be a lesser person without the kindness, practices, and works of the poets Eireann Lorsung, Rachel Moritz, and Stephanie Johnson. Thanks to Jim Cihlar and Bill Reichard for their input on earlier versions of the manuscript, and to Tony Frazer for publishing it. To Kathleen Coskran of the Malmo Art Colony and to the Blacklock Nature Sanctuary, thank you for the space to generate some of this work.

Lastly, a special kheili mamnoon to AG, without whom it doesn't mean much.

www.ingramcontent.com/pod-product-compliance
Lightning Source LLC
Chambersburg PA
CBHW031930080426
42734CB00007B/622

* 9 7 8 1 8 4 8 6 1 3 2 6 3 *